Robert Chambers

The Poetical Remains of Robert Chambers

Robert Chambers

The Poetical Remains of Robert Chambers

ISBN/EAN: 9783337777975

Printed in Europe, USA, Canada, Australia, Japan

Cover: Foto ©Thomas Meinert / pixelio.de

More available books at **www.hansebooks.com**

THE
POETICAL REMAINS

OF

ROBERT CHAMBERS, LL.D.

HOUSE AT PEEBLES IN WHICH ROBERT CHAMBERS WAS BORN.

EDINBURGH
1883

CONTENTS.

	PAGE
Introductory Notice,	7
The Grave of the Misanthrope,	9
Ennui,	11
Song, in the manner of the poets of the reign of Charles I.,	12
Polly Partan,	13
To the Evening Star,	15
My Native Bay,	16
Customer-Wark,	18
Verses,	22
To ————	23
Paraphrase of the First Ode of the Fourth Book of the *Odes* of Horace,	24
Mally Lee,	25
The Ladye that I Love,	27
To the Bell-Rock Lighthouse,	28
To Scotland,	29
O Maid Unloving,	33
Young Randal (*with Music*),	34
Lamente for the Aulde Hostels,	36
Sonnet to Lady Don,	40
Love Overhead,	41
Thou Gentle and Kind One (*with Music*),	44
On an Edition of Herrick's Select Poems,	46

CONTENTS.

	PAGE
Summer Evening, from Gavin Douglas,	47
Sonnet—'Like Precious Caskets,'	49
The Nook,	49
Lament for the Old Highland Warriors,	51
Fingask,	53
Lines to a Little Boy,	53
Absent Friends,	56
Embodying some Consequences of the Recent Disruption,	57
The Nine Holes of the Links of St Andrews,	58
The Peerless One,	63
On the Misses Threipland of Fingask going to see the Queen at Blair,	67
The Annuitant's Answer,	68
The Prisoner of Spedlins,	71
In the Album at Kinnaird Castle, Perthshire,	73
'All Right,'	74
On Seeing some Work-horses in a Park on a Sunday,	77
'Under Trustees,'	79
Elsinore,	81
Life Insurance,	83

INTRODUCTORY NOTICE.

THE present collection of poems, by the late Dr Robert Chambers, has been made partly from printed and partly from manuscript sources. In 1835, the author issued a small edition of his poems for private circulation; and that edition has been made the basis of the present, supplemented, however, by verse which has not previously appeared in print. Nearly all the pieces will be found to be characterised by the quaint kindly humour of the author of *Traditions of Edinburgh*. The poems written in 1821 originally appeared in the *Kaleidoscope*, a publication which was edited by the author and his brother, but did not long survive. One of the earliest ballads—that entitled Mally Lee—was composed from a song of the eighteenth century, the opening verse in each being identical. It was first published in the *Traditions of Edinburgh*. The name of the heroine was originally supposed to be Sleigh; and Allan Ramsay composed a poem, in 1724, in honour of the marriage of Lord Lyon Brodie and Mrs Mally Sleigh. Mr Charles Kirkpatrick Sharpe, however, in a letter to Dr Chambers, remarks that the name in the original manuscript, of which he had a copy, was Lee; and that 'Mally was a country beauty, and probably never in Edinburgh in her life.' An attempt is made in the ballad, by reference to costume and other circumstances, to awaken associations connected with Edinburgh in 1745.

The most important of the pieces composed since 1835 is, *The Annuitant's Answer*, a reply to George Outram's humorous verses, entitled *The Annuity*. Written in the Scottish dialect, the 'Answer' remained for a long time unpublished, but has latterly become better known, and is now included in various publications, among the latest being that of James Grant Wilson, on the *Poets and Poetry of Scotland*, where it is appended to *The Annuity*.

Dr Chambers, who was a great believer in the principles of Life Assurance, wrote some serio-comic verse on the subject; also a pamphlet, which at the time had a wide circulation. One of the best of the pieces is included in this collection, and has probably never before appeared in print.

Reference is made in several of the poems to personages at one time well known in Edinburgh literary society, but now almost forgotten. Among these we may mention Lady Don, very recently deceased; Sheriff Arkley, to whom the poem *Elsinore* was dedicated; and the Misses Threipland, with their brother, Sir Peter Murray Threipland of Fingask. Sir Peter survived his sisters a considerable time; and by his death, in 1882, a distinguished Jacobite family became extinct.

C. C.

EDINBURGH, *January* 1883.

POEMS.

THE GRAVE OF THE MISANTHROPE.

This poem relates to David Ritchie, a deformed and eccentric character, who, for many years previous to 1811, dwelt in a solitary cottage in the vale of Manor, near Peebles, and was allowed by Sir Walter Scott to have been the prototype of the fictitious character of the Black Dwarf. With an intellect of considerable native strength, and by no means uncultivated, this poor hater of his kind had a superstitious veneration for the mountain-ash, or rowan-tree, and his grave in Manor churchyard is marked by a plant of that species.

I sat upon the wizard's grave;
   'Twas on a smiling summer day,
When all around the desert spot
   Bloomed in the young delights of May.
In undistinguished lowliness,
   I found the little mound of earth;
And bitter weeds o'ergrew the place,
   As if his heart had given them birth.
And they from thence their nurture drew—
In such wild luxury they grew.

No friendship to his grave had lent
The rudely sculptured monument;
For he, the latest of his race,
Had left behind no friend to place

Such frail memorial o'er his breast
As marked the peasant's place of rest.
But o'er his head a sapling waved
   The honours of its slender form ;
And in its loneliness had braved
   The autumn's blast, the winter's storm ;
That drooping o'er that sod it might
   Repay a world's neglectful scorn,
And catching sorrow from the night,
   There weep a thousand tears at morn.
Some kindly hand the tribute gave,
To mark the undistinguished grave :
For it had been his favourite tree
In life, and haply still might be
A kindness to the spirit fled,
And ev'n in death might soothe the dead.

It was an emblem of himself,
   A widowed solitary thing,
To which no circling season might
   An hour of greener gladness bring.
A churchyard desert was its doom,
Its parent soil was all a tomb ;
There was it born, did live, will die ;
There will its withered ruins lie.
Such was the Solitary's fate,
So joyless and so desolate ;
For blasted soon as it was given,
   His was the life that had no hope ;
His was the soul that knew no heaven—
   Then, stranger, by one pitying drop,
   Forgive—forgive the Misanthrope.

1821.

ENNUI.

Written in a young lady's album—1821.

Oh, but I hate the tedious day,
Slow measuring out the idle hours,
When e'en enjoyment dies away,
In languishment that overpowers.
Life's gentle, dull, unvaried charms
Suit not with my distracted breast—
I'd love to be where raging storms
Might rock my furious soul to rest,
Wrapt in the blasting solitudes
Of tempests in their wildest moods.

I hate to linger on the shore;
When I might search the boundless sea,
And feel life's infant fears no more,
Swept on thy bounds, Eternity!
I scorn the rippling waves of time,
That kiss the level shores of life;
I'd love to see that other clime,
And hear that other ocean's strife,
Though 'twere to meet the fiery doom,
That was to sere and not consume.

I hate time's lazy noiseless foot,
That creeps so listlessly along;
I'd love through boundless worlds to shoot,
As lightning swift, as thunder strong.

While joy and grief, and hope and fear,
Compressed to ecstasy might seem;
And all existence but appear
One hurrying, wild, tempestuous dream;
A tempest-dream, that might not break,
Save at the words th' Eternal spake.

SONG.

In the manner of the poets of the Reign of Charles I.

Such thoughts as fairies dream,
Beside the haunted stream,
By moon-lit woods and solitudes,
Where nought of man may seem;

So bright as angels are,
When seen at morn afar,
In beauty laid on a golden bed,
Beneath the fading star;

Pure as that drop and true,
Where mimic forms we view,
So small, so bright, as exquisite—
A fairy world of dew!

Such thoughts, each beauty bright,
Such pureness exquisite,
To her belong of whom this song
My heart and harp indite.

1821.

POLLY PARTAN:

A BALLAD.

Before oysters became scarce, it was the habit of the Newhaven fishwomen to 'cry' them through the streets of Edinburgh. In those days, oysters were so plentiful that a hundred and twenty might be had for eightpence or a shilling; the musical cry of *Cailer Oo!* bringing joy to many a household. The following verses are in the author's happiest vein, and tell their own humorous story.

O pretty Polly Partan! she was a damsel gay,
And with a creel upon her back, she every night would stray
To the market-cross of Edinburgh, where singing she would stand,
While the gayest lords in Edinburgh ate oysters from her hand.

O such a beauty Polly was, she dang the fishwives a'—
Her cheek was like the partan's back, her nose was like its claw!
O how divinely did she look, when to her face there cam'
The blushes that accompany the taking of a dram!

Her love he was a sailor, a sailor on the sea,
And of a Greenland whaler the second mate was he;
But the Northern sea now covers him beneath its icy wave,
And the iceberg is the monument that lies upon his grave.

As pretty Polly Partan one night was going home,
And thinking of Tam Hallibuck and happy days to come,

Endeavouring to recollect if she was fou or not,
And counting that night's profits in her kilted petticoat;

She had not gone a mile, a mile down the Newhaven road,
When the spirit of Tam Hallibuck before poor Polly stood;
The hiccup rose unhiccuped through her amazed throat,
And the shilling dropt uncounted into her petticoat.

O cold turned Polly Partan; but colder was the ghost,
Who shivered in his shirt as folks are apt to do in frost;
And while from out his cheek he spat the phantom of a quid,
From the ghost of his tobacco-box he lifted off the lid.

'Oh! Polly,' cried the spirit, 'you may weep nae mair for me,
For my body it lies cauld and deep beneath the frozen sea;
Oh! will you be my bride, and go where sleeps your ain true lover?
The tangle-weed shall be your bed; the mighty waves, its cover.'

'O yes, I'll go!' cried Polly, 'for I can lo'e nane but you;'
And she turned into a spirit, and away with Tam she flew:
And in her track, far to the north, a ghastly light there shone;
Her *coats* were like the comet's tail, her fish-creel like the moon.

And some folk about Buckhaven, that were lecturing that night
On th' aurora borealis and its beauties all so bright,
Saw the spiritual lovers, with the lightning's quickest motion,
Shoot down among the streamers like two stars into the ocean.

1821.

TO THE EVENING STAR.

Soft star of eve, whose trembling light
   Gleams through the closing eve of day,
Where clouds of dying purple bright
   Melt in the shades of eve away,
And mock thee with a fitful ray,
   Pure spirit of the twilight hour,
Till forth thou blazeth to display
   The splendour of thy native power.

'Twas thus when earth from chaos sprung,
   The smoke of forming worlds arose,
And, o'er thine infant beauty hung,
   Hid thee awhile in dark repose;
Till the black veil dissolved away,
   Drunk by the universal air,
And thou, sweet star, with lonely ray,
   Shone out on paradise so fair.

When the first eve the world had known
   Fell blissfully on Eden's bowers,
And earth's first love lay couched upon
   The dew of Eden's fairest flowers;
Then thy first smile in heaven was seen
   To hail the birth of love divine,
And ever since that smile hath been
   The sainted passion's hallowed shrine:

Can lover yet behold thy beam
  Unmoved, unpassioned, unrefined?
While there thou shin'st the brightest gem,
  To night's cerulean crown assigned.

Since then, how many gentle eyes
  That love and thy pure ray made bright,
Have gazed on thee with wistful sighs—
  Now veiled in everlasting night!
Oh, let not love or youth be vain
  Of present bliss and hope more high;
The stars—the very clods remain—
  Love, they, and all of theirs must die.

Now throned upon the western wave,
  Thou tremblest coyly, star of love!
And dipp'st beneath its gleamy heave
  Thy silver foot, the bath to prove.
And though no power thy course may stay,
  Which nature's changeless laws compel,
To thee a thousand hearts may say—
  Sweet star of love, farewell, farewell!

1821.

MY NATIVE BAY.

My native bay is calm and bright,
  As e'er it was of yore,
When, in the days of hope and love,
  I stood upon its shore!

The sky is glowing soft and blue,
   As once in youth it smiled,
When summer seas and summer skies
   Were always bright and mild.

The sky, how oft hath darkness dwelt,
   Since then, upon its breast;
The sea, how oft have tempests woke
   Its billows from their rest!
So oft hath darker woe come o'er
   Calm self-enjoying thought;
And passion's storm a wilder scene
   Within my bosom wrought.

Now after years of absence, pass'd
   In wretchedness and pain,
I come, and find those seas and skies
   All calm and bright again;
The darkness and the storm from both
   Have trackless pass'd away;
And gentle as in youth once more
   Thou seem'st, my native bay!

O that, like thee, when toil is o'er,
   And all my griefs are past,
This ravaged bosom might subside
   To peace and joy at last!
And while it lay all calm like thee,
   In pure unruffled sleep,
Might then a heaven as bright as this
   Be mirrored in its deep!

1823.

CUSTOMER-WARK.*

In Ettrick's old vale, where the heather grows green,
Wi' aye here and there a bit plantin' between,
There lives an auld wabster, within an auld shiel,
As lang, and unchancy, and black as the deil.
He works e'en and morn for his wife and his weans,
Till the very flesh seems to be wrought frae his banes;
Yet canty's the wabster, and blyth as a lark,
Whene'er he gets what he ca's customer-wark!

This customer-wark's the delight o' his soul,
Whether blanket, or sheetin', or sarkin', or towel:
Nae trashtrie o' cottons frae Glasgow he cares for,
Their twopence the ell is a very good wherefore;

---

* In former times it was the custom all over Scotland for the housewife, assisted by her servants, and, in the case of the laird, by the wives and daughters of the tenantry, to spin as much woollen and linen yarn as sufficed to furnish clothes for her family, and napery for bed and board; a weaver being alone employed, besides, to put her handiwork into proper shape. Not long ago, a humble street in Edinburgh, called the Netherbow, was full of weavers of this kind; and as a proof of the extent to which the custom was carried two hundred years ago, even in the capital, I may mention that, when the Scottish Covenanters were about to invade England in 1640, the pious 'wives' of Edinburgh supplied them at a day's notice with a quantity of *harden*, a species of linen cloth, sufficient to furnish tents to the whole army, amounting to twenty thousand men.

In the present improved state of Scotland (1835), the division of labour system has, in a great measure, banished both the 'big' and the 'little' wheel; and, accordingly, there are not nearly so many weavers employed throughout the country, as used to be, in preparing cloth. Still, however, where such an individual is found, he is generally a more comfortable person than the muslin, or cotton weaver, who, in his labour, has to compete against the enormous odds of machinery, and is therefore, perhaps, the most abject and impoverished workman in the empire. Unfortunately, there are now very few *customer-weavers*, as they are called, who can obtain full employment; and, therefore, their existence is generally found to be one of comfort, chequered by intervals of penury.—*Note appended to the author's early edition.*

But God bless the wives, wi' their wheels and their thrift,
That help the poor wabster to fend and mak' shift;
Himsel', and his wife, and his weans might been stark,
An it hadna been them and their customer-wark.

The wabster's auld house is an unco-like den,
Though, atweel, like its neebors, it has a ben-en';
Its roof's just a hotter o' divots and thack,
Wi' a chimley dress'd up maist as big's a wheat-stack.
There's a peat-ruck behind, and a midden before,
And a jaw-hole would tak' a mile-race to jump o'er!
Ye may think him neglectfu' and lazy—but hark,
He's eydent eneuch at the customer-wark!

Whate'er ye may think him, the wabster's auld hut,
Has twa looms i' the ben, and twa beds i' the but,
A table, twa creepies, three chyres, and a kist,
And a settle to rest on whene'er that ye list;
The ben has a winnock, the but has a bole,
Where the bairns' parritch-luggies are set out to cool,
In providin' o' whilk he has mony a day's dargue
O' saxteen lang hours, at the customer-wark!

The wabster's auld madam—her name it is Bell—
Lang, ill-faured, and black, like the wabster himsel'—
She does nought the haill day but keeps skelpin' the bairns,
And hauds three or four o' them tight at the pirns.
Her tongue is as gleg and as sharp as a shuttle,
Whilk seldom but gies her the best o' the battle;
And sometimes her nieve lends the wabster a yerk,
That he likesna sae weel as his customer-wark!

The black cutty-pipe, that lies by the fireside,
Weel kens it the day when a wab has been paid,

For then wi' tobacco it's filled to the e'e,
And the wabster sits happy as happy can be;
For hours at a time it's ne'er out o' his cheek,
Till maist feck o' his winnings hae vanished in reek:
He says that o' life he could ne'er keep the spark,
An it werena the pipe and the customer-wark!

Then the wife, that's as fond o' her pleasure as he,
Brings out a black teapot and masks a drap tea;
And they sit, and they soss, and they haud a cabal,
Till ye think that their slaistrie wad never divaul.
By their wee spunk o' ingle they keep up the bother,
Each jeerin', misca'in', and scoldin' the tother;
While the bairns sit out by, wi' cauld kale, i' the dark—
Nae gude comes to them o' the customer-wark!

When the siller grows scarce, and the spleuchan gets toom,
The wabster gangs back to his treddles and loom,
Where he jows the day lang on some wab o' his ain,
That'll bring in nae cash for a twalmonth or twain;
Then the pipe is exhaustit and laid on the sill,
Though the fumes o' its sweetness will hang round it still,
And the teapot maun lie like a yaud in a park,
Till heaven shall neist send some customer-wark!

Then the puir starving wabster grows thinner and thinner,
On a 'tato for breakfast, a 'tato for dinner,
And vanishes veesibly, day after day,
Just like the auld moon when she eelies away.
Clean purged out he looks, like a worm amang fog,
And his face like a clatch o' auld sweens in a cogue.
At last, when grown hungry and gaunt as a shark,
He revives wi' a mouthfu' o' customer-wark!

A branksome gudewife, frae the neist farmer toun,
Comes in wi' a bundle, and clanks hersel' doun :
'How's a' wi' ye the day, Bell? Hae ye ought i' the pipe?
Come, rax me a stapper, the cutty I'll rype !
I maun see the gudeman—bring him ben, hinny Jess !
Tut ! the pipe's fu' o' naething but fizzenless asse !'
The wife ne'er lets on that she hears the remark,
But cries, 'Jess ! do ye hear, deme?—it's customer-wark !'

Having gotten her lick i' the lug, Jess gangs ben,
And tells her toom father about the God-sen';
Transported, he through the shop-door pops his head,
Like a ghaist glourin' out frae the gates o' the dead.
Then, wi' a great fraise he salutes the gudewife,
Says he ne'er saw her lookin' sae weel i' his life,
Spiers for the gudeman and the bairns at Glendeark,
While his thoughts a' the time are on customer-wark !

Then wi' the gudewife, he claps down on the floor,
And they turn and they count the haill yarn o'er and o'er :
He rooses her spinning, but canyells like daft
'Bout the length o' her warp and the scrimp o' her waft.
At last it's a' settled, and promised bedeen
To be ready on Friday or Fuirsday at e'en ;
And the bairns they rin out, wi' a great skirlin' bark,
To tell that their dad's got some customer-wark !

Then it's pleasant to see by the vera neist ouk,
How the wabster thowes out to his natural bouk,
How he freshens a thought on his diet o' brose,
And a wee tait o' colour comes back to his nose !
The cutty's new mountit, and everything's snug,
And Bell's tongue disna sing half sae loud i' his lug ;

Contented, and happy, and jum as a Turk,
He sits thinking on naething but customer-wark!

Oh, customer-wark! thou sublime moving spring!
It 's you gars the heart o' the wabster to sing!
An 'twerna for you, how puir were his cheer,
Ae meltith a day, and twa blasts i' the year:
It 's you that provides him the bit, brat, and beet,
And maks the twa ends o' the year sweetly meet,
That pits meat in his barrel, and meal in his ark—
My blessings gang wi' ye, dear customer-wark!

 1824.

VERSES.

We 'll flee to haunted woodlands,
 Thou dearest love of mine!
There greenwood deer may be our food,
 And crystal springs our wine;
Our bridal room shall be the sky,
 Which heav'n has drawn above,
With the bright moon to be alone
 The witness of our love.

We 'll flee to haunted woodlands,
 And leave this world of care;
Our love is of too pure a kind
 To be indulgèd there.
We 'll flee the face of scornful men,
 For they could ne'er approve
The pureness of our hallowed vow,
 The pureness of our love.

We 'll die in haunted woodlands,
  On some sweet eve we 'll die;
The gale that breathes from closing flowers
  Shall steal our latest sigh.
And when the autumn leaves shall fall,
  And o'er our bodies wither,
The fays that haunt the woodlands
  Shall cover us together.
1824.

TO ———

'Tis all too true—that faded cheek,
  That sunken eye,
Those accents tremulous and weak,
  That tear, that sigh.
With idle hope I 've watched thy brow
  From day to day;
'Tis vain—a little while, and thou
  Wilt pass away!

Nay, dear one! cease that soothing look,
  That soothing tone;
Thou dost not think that I could brook
  To be alone!
Thou wilt not say that I could bear
  On this dear spot
To seek thy footsteps everywhere,
  And find them not!

The sun will shine as bright above
  In other days;

The moon we used to watch and love
    Still win my gaze;
The flowers that shared thy gentlest care
    May still bloom on,
Our bird pour forth his song; but where
    Wilt thou be gone?

Mine eyes must close—where can they seek
    For aught so dear?
My lips be mute—why should I speak?
    Thou wilt not hear!
So, dearest! cease that soothing look,
    That soothing tone;
Thou dost not think that I could brook
    To be alone?

1825.

PARAPHRASE

OF THE FIRST ODE OF THE FOURTH BOOK OF THE 'ODES' OF HORACE.

Intermissa, Venus, diu rursus bella moves?
Parce, precor, precor———

Once more enchantress, wilt thou try
    Thoughts long subdued to move—
Cease, cease, I pray, nor think that I
    Again can ever love.

What once I was I am not now,
    Nor e'er shall be again,
Since years have left upon my brow
    Their tracks of grief and pain.

Go to the youth whose hourly prayers
    Are breathed before thy shrine,
And leave to its austerer cares
    This sullen heart of mine.

I see thee in the mazy dance
    To witching measures move,
I feel the lightning of thy glance—
    Yet cannot, cannot love.

Nor, though I might, could love avail
    To chain the flying hours;
As pulses in our temples fail,
    Though wreathed around with flowers.

Age now advances—loveless, vile,
    Cold, torpid, and severe—
When pleasure yields no grateful smile,
    Pain no relieving tear.

1825.

MALLY LEE.

As Mally Lee cam' doun the street, her capuchin did flee;
She cuist a look behind her, to see her negligee.
    And we're a' gaun east and west, we're a' gaun ajee;
    We're a' gaun east and west, courting Mally Lee.

She had lappets at her head, that flaunted gallantlie;
And ribbon-knots at back and breast of bonnie Mally Lee.
                And we're a' gaun, &c.

A' doun alang the Canongate were beaux o' ilk degree,
And mony ane turned round to look at bonnie Mally Lee.
      And we 're a' gaun, &c.

And ilka bab her pompoon gied, ilk lad thocht that 's to me ;
But ne'er a ane was in the thocht o' bonnie Mally Lee.
      And we 're a' gaun, &c.

Frae Seton's Land a countess fair look'd ower a window hie,
And pined to see the genty shape o' bonnie Mally Lee.
      And we 're a' gaun, &c.

And when she reached the Palace Porch, she met wi' yerls three,
And ilk ane thocht his Kate or Meg a drab to Mally Lee.
      And we 're a' gaun, &c.

The dance gaed through the palace ha', a comely sicht to see,
But nane was there sae bricht or braw as bonnie Mally Lee.
      And we 're a' gaun, &c.

Though some had jewels in their hair, like stars 'mang cluds did shine ;
Yet Mally far surpassed them a' wi' but her glancing eyne.
      And we 're a' gaun, &c.

A prince cam' out frae 'mang them a', wi' garter at his knee,
And danced a stately minuet wi' bonnie Mally Lee.
      And we 're a' gaun, &c.

1825.

THE LADYE THAT I LOVE.

Were I a doughty cavalier,
  On fire for high-born dame,
With sword and lance I would not fear
  To win a warrior's fame:
But since no more stern deeds of blood
  The gentle fair may move,
I'll woo in softer, better mood
  The ladye that I love.

For helmet bright with steel and gold,
  And plumes that flout the sky,
I'll wear a soul of hardier mould,
  And thoughts that sweep as high;
For scarf athwart my corslet cast,
  With her fair name y-wove,
I'll have her pictured in my breast,
  The ladye that I love.

No crested steed through battle throng
  Shall bear me bravely on;
But pride shall make my spirit strong,
  Where honours may be won:
Amidst the great of mind and heart,
  My prowess I will prove,
And thus I'll win by gentler art
  The ladye that I love.

1825.

TO THE BELL-ROCK LIGHTHOUSE.

Strange fancies rise at sight of thee,
Tower of the dim and silent sea.
Art thou a thing of earth or sky,
Upshot from beneath, or let down from on high,
A thing of the wave or a thing of the cloud,
The work of man or the work of God?
Old art thou—has thy blue minaret
Seen the young sons of creation set?
Or did but the yester years of time
Wake their old eyes on thy youthful prime,
Object of mystery sublime?

Strange are thy purposes and fate,
Emblem of all that's desolate.
Outcast of earth, as if cursed and exiled,
Thou hast taken thy place on the ocean wild,
And rear'st, like a mournful repentant Cain,
Thy conscious and flame-lettered brow on the main,
Telling all who might come to companion and cheer,
To shun thy abode of destruction and fear!

Hermit of the waste of sea,
Loneliest of all things that be,
The pillared fanatic was nothing to thee!
In calm and in sunshine, in gloom and in storm,
Thy constancy shrinks not, nor changes thy form;
Morn breaks on thy head with a blush and a smile,
Noon pours all his splendours around thy lone pile;

The long level sunbeams that gild thee at eve,
Cast thy shade till 'tis lost o'er the far German wave;
Or night falls upon thee, as dew falls on tree—
Yet these alternations no change bring to thee.

Let the sea, as the heaven which it mirrors, be calm,
And each breath of the breeze bring its own load of balm;
Or let this bleak pavement be traversed and torn
By those white-crested war-waves, on north-westers borne,
That seem, as they rush to old Albany's strand,
A new troop of Norsemen invading the land;
Or let the rough mood of this long-trooping host
In the madder conflict of the tempest be lost,
And to the wild scene deepest darkness be given,
Save where God pours his fire through the shot-holes of
    heaven,
In calm and in breeze, amidst tempest and flame,
Thou art still the same beautiful, terrible same!
    1826.

TO SCOTLAND.

Scotland! the land of all I love,
    The land of all that love me;
Land, whose green sod my youth has trod,
    Whose sod shall lie above me!
Hail, country of the brave and good,
    Hail, land of song and story;
Land of the uncorrupted heart,
    Of ancient faith and glory!

Like mother's bosom o'er her child,
    Thy sky is glowing o'er me;

Like mother's ever-smiling face,
    Thy land lies bright before me.
Land of my home, my father's land,
    Land where my soul was nourished ;
Land of anticipated joy,
    And all by memory cherished !

O Scotland, through thy wide domain,
    What hill, or vale, or river,
But in this fond enthusiast heart
    Has found a place for ever?
Nay, hast thou but a glen or shaw,
    To shelter farm or sheiling,
That is not garnered fondly up,
    Within its depths of feeling ?

Adown thy hills run countless rills,
    With noisy, ceaseless motion ;
Their waters join the rivers broad,
    Those rivers join the ocean :
And many a sunny, flowery brae,
    Where childhood plays and ponders,
Is freshened by the lightsome flood,
    As wimpling on it wanders.

Within thy long-descending vales,
    And on the lonely mountain,
How many wild spontaneous flowers
    Hang o'er each flood and fountain !
The glowing furze—the 'bonny broom,'
    The thistle, and the heather ;
The blue-bell, and the gowan fair,
    Which childhood loves to gather.

Oh, for that pipe of silver sound,
  On which the shepherd lover,
In ancient days, breathed out his soul,
  Beneath the mountain's cover !
Oh, for that Great Lost Power of Song,
  So soft and melancholy,
To make thy every hill and dale
  Poetically holy !

And not alone each hill and dale,
  Fair as they are by nature,
But every town and tower of thine,
  And every lesser feature ;
For where is there the spot of earth,
  Within my contemplation,
But from some noble deed or thing
  Has taken consecration ?

First, I could sing how brave thy sons,
  How pious and true-hearted,
Who saved a bloody heritage
  For us in times departed ;
Who, through a thousand years of wrong,
  Oppressed and disrespected,
Ever the generous, righteous cause
  Religiously protected.

I 'd sing of that old early time,
  When came the victor Roman,
And, for the first time, found in them
  Uncompromising foemen ;
When that proud bird, which never stooped
  To foe, however fiery,
Met eagles of a sterner brood
  In this our northern eyry.

Next, of that better glorious time,
    When thy own patriot Wallace
Repell'd and smote the myriad foe
    Which stormed thy mountain palace;
When on the sward of Bannockburn
    De Bruce his standard planted,
And drove the proud Plantagenet
    Before him, pale and daunted.

Next, how, through ages of despair,
    Thou brav'dst the English banner,
Fighting like one who hopes to save
    No valued thing but honour.
How thy own young and knightly kings,
    And their fair hapless daughter,
Left but a tale of broken hearts
    To vary that of slaughter.

How, in a later, darker time,
    When wicked men were reigning,
Thy sons went to the wilderness,
    All but their God disdaining;
There, hopeful only of the grave,
    To stand through morn and even,
Where all on earth was black despair,
    And nothing bright but heaven.

And, later still, when times were changed,
    And tend'rer thoughts came o'er thee,
When abject, suppliant, and poor,
    Thy injurer came before thee,
How thou did'st freely all forgive,
    Thy heart and sword presented,

Although thou knew'st the deed must be
    In tears of blood repented.

Scotland! the land of all I love,
    The land of all that love me;
Land, whose green sod my youth has trod,
    Whose sod shall lie above me;
Hail! country of the brave and good,
    Hail! land of song and story,
Land of the uncorrupted heart,
    Of ancient faith and glory!

1826.

O MAID UNLOVING.

O maid unloving, but beloved,
    My soul's unchanging theme,
Who art by day my only thought,
    By night my only dream;
Thou think'st not, in thy pride of place,
    When gay ones bow the knee,
How bends one lonely distant heart,
    In earnest love of thee.

As ancient worshippers but knew
    One attitude of prayer,
And turning to the holy east,
    Pour'd all their spirit there;
So to thy home inclines this heart,
    All distant though it be,
And knows but one adoring art,
    An earnest love of thee.

1826.

YOUNG RANDAL.

Air—*There grows a bonnie brier bush in our kail-yard.*

YOUNG RANDAL.

A BALLAD.

Young Randal was a bonnie lad, when he gaed awa',
Young Randal was a bonnie lad, when he gaed awa';
'Twas in the sixteen hunder year o' grace and thretty-twa,
That Randal, the laird's youngest son, gaed awa'.

It was to seek his fortune in the High Germanie,
To fecht the foreign loons in the High Germanie,
That he left his father's tower o' sweet Willanslee,
And mony wae friends i' the North Countrie.

He left his mother in her bower, his father in the ha',
His brother at the outer yett, but and his sisters twa,
And his bonnie cousin Jean, that looked owre the castle wa',
And, mair than a' the lave, loot the tears doun fa'.

'Oh, whan will ye be back?' sae kindly did she spier,
'Oh, whan will ye be back, my hinny and my dear?'
'Whenever I can win eneuch o' Spanish gear,
To dress ye out in pearlins and silks, my dear.'

Oh, Randal's hair was coal black, when he gaed awa',
Oh, Randal's cheeks were roses red, when he gaed awa',
And in his bonnie e'e, a spark glintit high,
Like the merrie, merrie lark, in the morning sky.

Oh, Randal was an altert man when he came hame,
A sair altert man was he, when he came hame,
Wi' a ribbon at his breast, and a *sir* at his name,
And gray, gray cheeks, did Randal come hame.

He lichtit at the outer yett, and rispit wi' the ring,
And down came a ladye to see him come in,
And after the ladye came bairns fciftcen—
'Can this muckle wife be my true love, Jean?'

'Whatna stoure carle is this?' quo' the dame;
'Sae gruff and sae grand, and sae feckless and sae lame?'
'Oh, tell me, fair madam, are ye bonnie Jeanie Grahame?'
'In troth,' quo' the ladye, 'sweet sir, the very same.'

He turned him about, wi' a waeful e'e,
And a heart as sair as sair could be;
He lap on his horse, and awa' did wildly flee,
And never mair came back to sweet Willanslee.

Oh, dule on the poortith o' this countrie,
And dule on the wars o' the High Germanie,
And dule on the love that forgetfu' can be—
For they 've wrecked the bravest heart in this hale countrie!
   1827.

LAMENTE FOR THE AULD HOSTELS.*

'Oh, Edinbruch, hich and triumphand toun,
   Within thy bounds rycht merrie haif I bene!'
Sae said Schir David Lyndsay, that slie loun,
   Wha kenned what merrines wes rycht weil, I wene;

---

* The author must be understood in this piece to speak poetically, not literally.

And sae say I, that mony a bouse haif sene,
In quyet houses round about the Croce
   (Haplie now herboure for the vyle and meane),
In the Hie Streit, or als in wynde or closse,
Renowned for punche and aill, and eke hie-relished soss.

But now, alas for thee, decayit Dunedin,
   Thy dayis of glory are departit quite ;
For all those places that we ance were fed in,
   And where we decently gotte foue o' night,
Those havens of douce comforte and delighte,
   Are closed, degraded, burnt, or changed, or gone,
Whyle our old hostesses have ta'en their flight,
To far-off places, novel and unknowne,
About whose verie names we skairslie may depone.

Whair now is Douglas's? whair Clerihugh's?
   Whair is John's Coffee-house? and tell me whair
Is Mistress P——'s? to which, when these old shoes
   Were new, at eight we used to make repair ;
By her own ladye hand showne up the staire,
   Through a long trance, into a panyled roome
Whair lords had erst held feist wyth ladyes faire,
And which had still an air of lordly gloome,
That scarss two sturdie mouldes colde utterlie illume.

Oh for the pen of Fergusson to painte
   'The parloure splendours of that festyf place !'
The niche, sumtyme the shrine of sum old sainte,
   The ceilyng that still bore, in antique grace,
   Many a holye, chubby, white-washt face ;
The dark-brown landscape, done of old by Norie,
   On the broad panel o'er the chimney-brace ;

The blue-tiled fireplace gleamyng in its glorye,
Relating, verse for verse, sum morall Scrypture storye.

Then on the wall was hung that rare and rych
    Memoriall of a tyme and mode gone by,
The *samplar*, showing every kind of stitch
    E'er known or practised underneath the skye—
    Thread-circled holes denominated ' pye '—
Embattled lynes—of squayr-tayled lambs a paire—
    Strange cloven-footed letters awkwardlye
Contriving to make up the Lorde hys prayer—
And names of John and Jean and William all were thair.

Thair, also, hung around the wainscot wall,
    Eche in its panel, of old prynts a store ;
Adam in paradyce before the Falle ;
    The sailors mutinying at the Nore ;
    Flora—Pomona—and the sesons four ;
Lord Nelson's victory at Trafalgar ;
    The deth of Cooke on Otaheite's shore ;
Lord North rigged out in gartyr and in star ;
With manie more ta'en out of Historie of the Warre.

Then thair were tablis, also, squayr and round,
    Derke as the face of old antiquity,
Yet, when inspected, each a mirror found,
    So that ilke feature you full well could spye ;
    The jugges and glasses on those planes did lye,
Lyke summer barkes in glassye seas reflected ;
    And chayrs were thair, as vertical and high
As the proude race upoun them once erected,
In each of whome, 'tis sayd, ane pokyr was injected.

But ah ! the mere externe of this olde haunte—
    Preciouse althoughe in everye lineamente—

Wes the leaste worthie subject of descante ;
  The sorrow which mine anxious muse wolde vent,
  Regairds alone the happy moments, spente
Sae cozilie within that humble dome,
  In nights of other years—jocoseness blente
With courtesie—the decencies of home—
Yet o'er the realmes of talke for ever frie to roame.

To me who love the olde with such regrette,
  What charme can be apparent in the newe?
Divans, saloons, and café's may besette
  The heartes of youth, and seem to fancye's viewe
Places more fit to lounge in, while the stewe
Of numbers has a charme ; but oh, how far
  From hearty is the pleasance they pursue—
Eche manne his single rummyr and cigarre,
Puffing, all by himself—a sulky, smoky warre !

Bot vayne it is to sorrow for the paste—
  Dunedin stands not now quhair once it stoode :
Ilke thing of old is hastenyng from it faste,
  And bridges it must haif, althoch no floode ;
  The auld wes cozie, and the auld wes goode,
And Mistress P—— of hosteleres wes the quene ;
  Bot dinging down is now the reigning moode,
And auld-town hostels are extynguyshed clene—
I haif, in troth, ane end of al perfectioun sene.*
  1828.

---

* When some one made inquiry of Nanse Tinnock of Mauchline, respecting the convivial habits of Robert Burns—which, it was presumed, she must have had the best opportunities of observing—the old lady answered that she really could say little upon the subject, 'as the chield had hardly ever drunk twa half-mutchkins in her house.' If any one presume from the above poem, that the author must have been well acquainted, personally, with the taverns of ancient Edinburgh, and entered largely into the festivities practised in them,

SONNET TO LADY DON.

The lady to whom the accompanying sonnet is addressed was, sixty years ago, considered the most beautiful woman in the Scottish capital. She was the daughter of Mr John Stein of Edinburgh, and first married Sir Alexander Don, Bart., by whom she had a son, Sir William H. Don, at one time well known as the baronet actor; and a daughter, the wife of Sir F. A. Millbank, Bart., M.P. for the North Riding of Yorkshire. Lady Don married, secondly, Lieutenant-general Sir James Maxwell Wallace; and died, at an advanced age, on the 13th of March 1878.

Lady, thou wert not formed for this cold clime,
  Nor for this tame and unchivalric age;
  Thou 'rt all misplaced upon this humble stage,
Thou hast come to the world *behind* thy time.
Thou should'st have lived five hundred years agone,
In some lone castle near the proud Garonne,
With such concourse of lovers from all Spain,
That towns at length should rise on thy domain;
Kings should come there to break their hearts in scores,
  And thou should'st hold a massacre of knights
Once every week, until the river's shores
  Should peopled be with their untimely sprites.
Thou should'st lay waste a kingdom with thy charms,
And yield to none but Death's all-conquering arms.

1829.

a mistake will be committed not less than that of the individual who applied to the Mauchline hostess for the bacchanalian character of Burns. He only once or twice saw scenes such as are here described; and as a further illustration of the fallacy of reasoning from print to its author, it occurred to him that, notwithstanding the minute information given in the *Traditions of Edinburgh* regarding clubs, he never, up to that time, and for some years later, happened to be once present at the meeting of any such fraternity.

LOVE OVERHEAD.

Some people say they nothing love
   In woman, save the sacred mind,
Pretending in her boasted form,
   No charm of merit they can find.

Others—and this in Thomson's school—
   Are all for beauty unadorned,
Caring small things, 'twould seem, for soul,
   And holding dress but to be scorned.

Away with all such saving clauses!
   I love my Julia altogether,
From soul within to silk without,
   From point of toe to top of feather.

Her dear idea is to me
   One lustrous silhouette of light,
Where every edge of lace and frill
   Is as the inmost core as bright.

For instance, now, I love her eyes,
   So dark, yet dove-like in expression;
Yet to the pendants at her ears,
   My eyes will sometimes make digression.

Her cheeks are like the roses red,
   Her mouth is like the parted cherry;
But don't these combs become her much?
   Are they not charming? Yes, oh very!

Her head moves with a queenly grace;
   A crown would not look queer upon it;
But, in the meantime, is not this
   A very tasteful sort of bonnet?

Her hands are soft and paly white,
   Her fingers tapering, small, and seemly;
But oh, her bracelets and her gloves,
   I love them, love them most extremely.

Her feet so gentle are and small,
   They give a grace to shoe and stocking;
Shoe, stocking, foot—'tis but one thing,
   That sets this foolish heart a-knocking.

I am of Hudibras's thought,
   Who looked on 't as a sort of duty,
While he admired his fair one's face,
   T' adore the shade even of her shoe-tye.

I wear a tassel from her gown,
   Snug near my heart in left vest-pocket;
I have a ringlet of her hair,
   Hung not more near it in a locket.

Her parasol, that from the sun
   Protects her roseate complexion,
I don't know which I love the most,
   The thing that takes or gives protection.

The thrilling music of her voice
   Puts all my senses in a tussle;
And every nerve springs up to hear
   Her distant bombazines play rustle.

Whate'er she does, whate'er she says,
  For good, indifferent, or ill,
'Tis all one luxury to my soul,
  'Tis Julia yet, 'tis Julia still.

Say that she talks of mutual love,
  And puts her poor swain in a rapture;
Say that she tells her kitchen-maid
  To make in poultry-yard a capture;

Say that she reads some touching tale,
  That gems with tears her soft eye-lashes;
Say that she pities but the scribe
  Whom some fell critic cuts and slashes;

'Tis all one thing—mind, person, dress—
  The formed of heaven, or dust, or shears—
I love the whole, and nothing less;
  I love her overhead—and ears.

1829.

THOU GENTLE AND KIND ONE.

Air—*My Nannie's awa.*

Thou gen-tle and kind one, who com'st o'er my dreams, Like gales of the west, or the mu-sic of streams; Oh, soft-est and dear-est, can that time e'er be, When I'll be for-get-ful or scorn-ful of thee? When

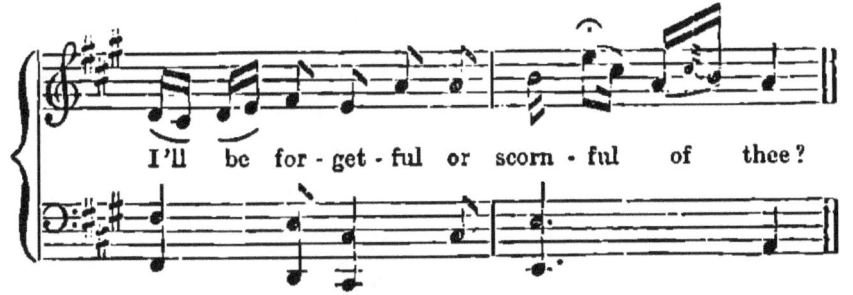

THOU GENTLE AND KIND ONE.

Thou gentle and kind one,
    Who com'st o'er my dreams,
Like the gales of the west,
    Or the music of streams;
Oh, softest and dearest
    Can that time e'er be,
When I could be forgetful
    Or scornful of thee?

No! my soul might be dark,
    Like a landscape in shade,
And for thee not the half
    Of its love be displayed.
But one ray of thy kindness
    Would banish my pain,
And soon kiss every feature
    To brightness again.

And if in contending
    With men and the world,
My eye might be fierce
    Or my brow might be curled.

That brow on thy bosom
   All smoothed would recline,
And that eye melt in kindness
   When turned upon thine.

If faithful in sorrow,
   More faithful in joy—
Thou should'st find that no change
   Could affection destroy;
All profit, all pleasure,
   As nothing would be,
And each triumph despised,
   Unpartaken by thee.

1829.

ON AN EDITION OF HERRICK'S SELECT POEMS.

Being an imitation of the manner of that Poet.

A tiny tome, such as might lie
In Mistress Mab's own library;
With boards of rose and leaves of cream,
And little print that might beseem
The footmarks of the fairy throng,
As o'er a snow-charged leaf they lightly tripped along.

Oh, if to Herrick's sainted mind
Aught earthly now its way can find,
Be this sweet book-flower softly shed,
By fays, upon his last green bed!

'Twill mind him of those things he loved,
When he the sweet-breathed country roved,
Inside he'll find his own pure lilies,
Outside his golden daffodillies ;
On every leaf some lovesome thing
Back to his shade life's thoughts will bring.
Here Phillis with her pastoral messes,
And Julia with her witching dresses ;
There daisies from a hundred hills
And crystal from a thousand rills
(Rills whose every trinkling fall
With nightingales is musical) ;
And posies all around beset
With primrose and rich violet ;
And robes beneath the cestus thrown
Into a fine distraction ;
And ladies' lips, which sweetly smile,
Among the groves of Cherry Isle.

1830.

SUMMER EVENING.

An Anglo-Scottish version of a passage in Gavin Douglas.

'Twas in the jolly joyous month of June,
When gane was near the day and supper dune,
I walkit furth to taste the evening air,
Among the fields that were replenished fair
With herbage, corn, and cattle, and fruit-trees,
Plenty of store ; while birds and busy bees
O'er emerald meadows flew baith east and west,
Their labour done to take their evening rest.

As up and down I cast my wandering eye,
All burning red straight grew the western sky ;
The sun, descending on the waters gray,
Deep under earth withdrew his beams away ;
The evening star with growing lustre bright,
Sprung up, the gay fore-rider of the night ;
Amid the haughs and every pleasant vale,
The recent dew began on herbs to skail ;
The light began to dim, and mists to rise,
And here and there grim shades o'erspread the skies ;
The bald and leathern bat commenced her flight,
The lark descended from her airy height ;
Mists swept the hill before the lazy wind,
And night spread out her cloak with sable lined,
Swaddling the beauty of the fruitful ground
With cloth of shade, obscurity profound.
All creatures, wheresoe'er they liked the best,
Then went to take their pleasant nightly rest.
The fowls that lately wantoned in the air,
The drowsy cattle in their sheltered lair,
After the heat and labour of the day,
Unstirring and unstirred in slumber lay.
Each thing that roves the meadow or the wood,
Each thing that flies through air or dives in flood,
Each thing that nestles in the bosky bank,
Or loves to rustle through the marshes dank,
The little midges and the happy flees,
Laborious emmets, and the busy bees,
All beasts, or wild or tame, or great or small,
Night's peace and blessing rests serene o'er all.

1832.

SONNET.

Like precious caskets in the deep sea casten,
On which the clustering shell-fish quickly fasten,
   Till closed they seem in chinkless panoplie ;
So do our hearts, into this world's moil thrown,
Become with self's vile crust straight overgrown,
   Of which there scarce may any breaking be.
So may not mine, though quick-setted all round
   With sternest cares : still for the young departed,
   And more for the surviving broken-hearted,
For all who sink beneath affliction's wound,
May I at least some grief or pity feel :
   Still let my country and my kindred's name,
   Still let religion's mild and tender flame,
Have power to move : I would not all be steel.

1833.

THE NOOK.

Iste terrarum mihi, præter omnes,
Angulus ridet.
                HORACE.

(Written during a visit at the Nook, near Airth, Stirlingshire.)

One thing seems agreed on in speech and in book,
That, if comfort exists, 'twill be found in a nook ;
All seems dreary and cold in an open area,
But a corner—how charming the very idea !

Hence, when weary with toiling, we think of retreat,
A nook is the place that we ask for our seat—
Some small piece of earth, 'tis no matter how small,
But a corner it must be, or nothing at all.
The poor man an object of kindred desire
Regards, in the nook of his bright evening fire,
Where, his labours all done, he may sit at his ease,
With his wee things devoutly caressing his knees;
And where, I would know, to what promising shade,
Runs the kiss-threatened, bashful, yet half-willing maid?
To some nook, to be sure, to some hidden recess,
Where her lover his fondness is free to confess.
Even less might have been the delight of Jack Horner,
Had his plums been enjoyed anywhere but a corner!

Since thus open pleasures are viler than tangle,
And true ones, like trout, must be caught by the angle,
Perfect joy, it seems clear, must by hook or by crook,
Be obtained in a place called, *par excellence*, NOOK.
The Nook!—how endearing and pleasant the word—
As bieldy and warm as the nest of a bird!
Sure a place so designed must know little care,
And summer must linger eternally there;
No resting-place, surely, for sorrow or sin,
But all blossom without and all pleasure within:
There children must sport, all unknowing of pain,
And old folk, looking on, become children again.
Sad Poortith will pass it ungrudgingly by,
And wealth only cast a solicitous eye.
'Twere surely fit scene for a goddess' descent—
The goddess long lost to us—holy Content.
Such thoughts it is easy to string up together;
But reason might smash them perhaps with a feather,

And things might be in such a concatenation,
That the nook might become quite a scene of vexation.
Yet of this, as it happens, there's no chance or little,
Unless, like the smallpox, vexation turns smittle;
For here lives good ——, the blithest and best,
Who is happy himself and makes happy the rest,
Whose temper is such, as he proves by his look,
That joy would be with him, *even not in a nook;*
Who has wit for all topics, and worth with it all,
And, while mirth is in presence, keeps sense within call.
To the Nook, why, a man such as this is as pat,
As the foot to the shoe, or the head to the hat;
And so well do they answer to each other's quality,
So mixed is the man with his pleasant locality,
That a question it seems, and I cannot decide it,
Whether he or the Nook gives the most of the 'ridet.'

1834.

LAMENT FOR THE OLD HIGHLAND WARRIORS.

Air—*Cro Challein.**

Oh where are the pretty men of yore,
　Oh where are the brave men gone,
Oh where are the heroes of the north?
　Each under his own gray stone.
Oh where now the broad bright claymore,
　Oh where are the truis and plaid?

---

* Cro Challein is the name of a remarkably mournful Highland song, which, according to tradition, originated with the spirit of a farmer's wife, who was heard singing to her husband's cattle some months after her death. The air is to be found in *A Selection of Celtic Melodies* (Edinburgh: Purdie, 1830).

Oh where now the merry Highland heart?
  In silence for ever laid.

    Och on a rie, och on a rie,
      Och on a rie, all are gone,
    Och on a rie, the heroes of yore,
      Each under his own gray stone.

The chiefs that were foremost of old,
  Macdonald and brave Lochiel,
The Gordon, the Murray, and the Graham,
  With their clansmen true as steel ;
Who followed and fought with Montrose,
  Glencairn, and bold Dundee,
Who to Charlie gave their swords and their all,
  And would aye rather fa' than flee.

    Och on a rie, och on a rie,
      Och on a rie, all are gone,
    Och on a rie, the heroes of yore,
      Each under his own gray stone.

The hills that our brave fathers trod,
  Are now to the stranger a store ;
The voice of the pipe and the bard
  Shall waken never more.
Such things it is sad to think on—
  They come like the mist by day—
And I wish I had less in this world to leave,
  And be with them that are away.

    Och on a rie, och on a rie,
      Och on a rie, all are gone,
    Och on a rie, the heroes of yore,
      Each under his own gray stone.

1835.

FINGASK.*

Fair perched upon the woody mountain's brow,
   Amidst the devious rush of Alpine rills—
   A jewel in the bosom of the hills—
I see Fingask, that gallant old chateau !
Seat in past time of many a loyal heart,
   Which, every thought of self behind it throwing,
   And with a generous patriot spirit glowing,
In Stuart cause performed a noble part !
The home even yet of ancient love and faith,
And loyalty that would be true till death,
   Where beauty, honour, wit, and goodness dwell,
What better can I say, fair spot of earth,
Than that each parting pilgrim of thy hearth,
   Like me may sigh to give thee his farewell.

1836.

LINES TO A LITTLE BOY.

My winsome one, my handsome one, my darling little boy,
The heart's pride of thy mother, and thy father's chiefest joy ;
Come ride upon my shoulder, come sit upon my knee,
And prattle all the nonsense that I love to hear from thee :
With thine eyes of merry lustre, and thy pretty lisping tongue,
And thy heart that evermore lets out its humming happy song :

---

* The seat of the Threiplands, a memorable Jacobite family. Sir P. Murray Threipland, the last Baronet, died in 1882.

With thy thousand tricks so gleesome, which I bear without
    annoy,
Come to my arms, come to my soul, my darling little boy!

My winsome one, my fairest one, they say that later years
Will sometimes change a parent's hope for bitter grief and
    tears :
But *thou*, so innocent! canst thou be aught but what thou
    art,
And all this bloom of feeling with the bloom of face depart?
Canst thou this tabernacle fair, where God reigns bright
    within,
Profane, like Judah's children, with the Pagan rites of sin?
No—no;'so much I'll cherish thee, so clasped we'll be
    in one,
That bugbear guilt shall only get the father with the son ;
And thou, perceiving that the grief must *me* at least destroy,
Wilt still be fair and innocent, my darling little boy!

My gentle one, my blessed one, can that time ever be,
When I to thee shall be severe, or thou unkind to me?
Can any change which time may bring, this glowing passion
    wreck,
Or clench with rage the little hand now fondling round my
    neck?
Can this community of sport, to which love brings me down,
Give way to anger's kindling glance, and hate's malignant
    frown?
No—no, that time can ne'er arrive, for, whatsoe'er befall,
This heart shall still be wholly thine, or shall not be at all ;
And to an offering like this thou canst not e'er be coy,
But still wilt be my faithful and my gentle little boy!

My winsome one, my gallant one, so fair, so happy now,
With thy bonnet set so proudly upon thy shining brow,
With thy fearless bounding motions, and thy laugh of
    thoughtless glee,
So circled by a father's love which wards each ill from thee !
Can I suppose another time when this shall all be o'er,
And thy cheek shall wear the ruddy badge of happiness
    no more :
When all who now delight in thee far elsewhere shall have
    gone,
And thou shalt pilgrimise through life, unfriended and alone,
Without an aid to strengthen or console thy troubled mind,
Save the memory of the love of those who left thee thus
    behind?
Oh, let me not awake the thought, but, in the present blest,
Make thee a child of wisdom—and to Heaven bequeath
    the rest :

Far rather let me image thee, in sunny future days,
Outdoing every deed of mine, and wearing brighter bays ;
With less to dull thy fervency of recollected pain,
And more to animate thy course of glory and of gain ;
A home as happy shall be thine, and I too shall be there,
The blessings purchased by thy worth in peace and love
    to share—
Shall see within thy beaming eye my early love repaid,
And every ill of failing life a bliss by kindness made—
Shall see thee pour upon thy son, then sitting on thy knee,
A father's gushing tenderness, such as I feel for thee ;
And know, as I this moment do, no brighter, better joy,
Than thus to clasp unto thy soul thy darling little boy !

ABSENT FRIENDS.

Air—*The Peacock.*

The night has flown wi' sangs and glee,
    The minutes ha'e like moments been—
There's friendship's spark in ilka e'e,
    And peace has blessed the happy scene.
But while we sit sae social here,
    And think sic friends we never saw,
Let's not forget, for them that's near,
    The mony mae that's far awa'.

Oh, far beyond th' Atlantic's roar,
    Far, far beyond th' Australian main,
How many Fortune's ways explore,
    That we may never meet again!
How many ance sat by our side,
    Or danced beside us in the ha',
Wha wander now the world sae wide—
    Let's think on them that's far awa'.

There's no a mother but has seen,
    Through tears, her manly laddies gae;
There's no a lass but thinks o' ane
    Whase absence makes her aften wae;
The ingle sides o'er a' the land,
    They now are dowf and dowie a',
For some ane o' the social band
    Has left them, and is far awa'.

They 've left us—but, where'er they be,
    They ne'er forget their native shore ;
Auld Scotland, mountain, glen, and lea,
    They have it pictured at the core ;
E'en now, when we remember them,
    Our memory they perhaps reca',
And when we fondly breathe their name,
    They whisper ours, though far awa'.

1839.

EMBODYING SOME CONSEQUENCES OF THE RECENT DISRUPTION.

The women are a' gane wud,
    They've gotten a terrible thraw ;
And Candlish is the lad
    Has pushioned their judgments a'.

Tam Jobson was a man
    That lived a peaceable life,
But now he rest gets nane
    For his daughters and his wife.

They deave him about the kirk,
    Which they Erastian ca' ;
For naething will satisfy them
    But the kirk that's against the law.

And sae while he, douce man,
    Sits doun in his ain auld seat,
They're aff to some muirside tent,
    And winna be hame *till late*.

They gang frae house to house,
  Wi' mony a wile and quirk,
Frae puir folk forcing cash
  To uphaud the *spontaneous kirk*.

Tam says they'll break his heart,
  They tell him it just maun be,
For they maun do what's right,
  Though father or husband *die*.

Atweel, an the case were mine,
  I'd tell them a bit o' my mind,
And, failing effect o' words,
  I'd lay on a stick behind.

The women are a' gane wud,
  They've gotten a terrible thraw;
And Candlish is the lad
  Has pushioned their judgments a'.

1844.

THE NINE HOLES OF THE LINKS OF ST ANDREWS.

IN A SERIES OF VERSES.

For the benefit of those who may be uninitiated in the mysteries and in the delights of Golf, Scotland's national game, it may be well to mention that St Andrews has always been its headquarters. The Links, which extend from the town to the river Eden, a distance of several miles, are admirably adapted, from the close texture of the grass, for the pastime, and comprise eighteen holes in all, that is to say, nine 'out' and nine 'in.' Each hole and the intervening ground between has its characteristic features, and these are in a measure portrayed in the following verses. The first three sonnets are from the pen of Dr Robert Chambers; the next three are by Mr P. P. Alexander; the last three, by Mr Robert Chambers, son of the above.

I. THE FIRST OR BRIDGE HOLE.

Sacred to hope and promise is the spot—
    To Philp's[1] and to the Union Parlour[2] near,
    To every golfer, every caddie dear—
Where we strike off—oh, ne'er to be forgot,
Although in lands most distant we sojourn.
    But not without its perils is the place;
    Mark the opposing caddie's[3] sly grimace,
Whispering: 'He's on the road!' 'He's in the burn!'
So is it often in the grander game
    Of life, when, eager, hoping for the palm,
Breathing of honour, joy, and love, and fame,
    Conscious of nothing like a doubt or qualm.
We start, and cry: 'Salute us, muse of fire!'
And the first footstep lands us in the mire.

II. THE SECOND OR CARTGATE HOLE.

Fearful to Tyro is thy primal stroke,
    O Cartgate, for behold the bunker[4] opes
    Right to the *teeing*[5] place its yawning chops,
Hope to engulf ere it is well awoke.
That passed, a Scylla in the form of rushes
    Nods to Charybdis which in ruts appears:
    He will be safe who in the middle steers;
One step aside, the ball destruction brushes.
Golf symbols thus again our painful life,
    Dangers in front, and pitfalls on each hand:
    But see, one glorious cleek-stroke[6] from the sand
Sends Tyro home, and saves all further strife!

He's in at six—old Sandy[7] views the lad
With new respect, remarking : 'That's no bad !'

III. THE THIRD HOLE.

No rest in golf—still perils in the path :
    Here, playing a good ball, perhaps it goes
    Gently into the *Principalian Nose*,[8]
Or else *Tam's Coo*, which equally is death.
Perhaps the wind will catch it in mid-air,
    And take it to *the Whins*—' Look out, look out !
    Tom Morris,[9] be, O be a faithful scout !'
But Tom, though *links-eyed*, finds 't not anywhere.
Such thy mishaps, O Merit : feeble balls
    Meanwhile roll on, and lie upon the green ;
'Tis well my friends, if you, when this befalls,
    Can spare yourselves the infamy of spleen.
It only shows the ancient proverb's force,
That you may further go and fare the worse.

IV. THE FOURTH OR GINGER-BEER HOLE.

Though thou hast lost this last unlucky hole,
    I say again, betake thee not to swearing,
    Or any form of speech profanely daring,
Though some allege it tendeth to console.
Better do thou thy swelling griefs control,
    Sagacious that at hand a joy awaits thee
    (Since out of doubt a glass of beer elates thee),
Without that frightful peril to thy soul.
A glass of beer ! go dip thine angry beak in it,
    And straight its rage will melt to soft placidity,
That solace finding thou art wise to seek in it ;
    Ah, do not thou on this poor plea reject it,

That in thy inwards it will breed acidity—
    One glass of Stewart's brandy will correct it.

V. THE HELL HOLE.

What daring genius first yclept thee Hell?
    What high, poetic, awe-struck grand old golfer,
    Much more of a mythologist than scoffer!
Whoe'er he was, the name befits thee well.
'All hope abandon, ye who enter here,'
    Is written awful o'er thy gloomy jaws,
    A threat to all save Allan might give pause:
And frequent from within come tones of fear—
Dread sound of cleeks, which ever fall in vain,
    And—for mere mortal patience is but scanty—
Shriekings thereafter, as of souls in pain,
    Dire gnashings of the teeth, and horrid curses,
    With which I need not decorate my verses,
Because, in fact, you'll find them all in Dante.

VI. THE HEATHER HOLE.

Ah me, prodigious woes do still environ—
    To quote verbatim from some grave old poet—
The man who needs must meddle with his *iron*,[10]
    And here, if ever, thou art doomed to know it.
For now behold thee, doubtless for thy sins,
    Tilling some bunker, as if on a lease of it,
    And so assiduous to make due increase of it,
Or wandering homeless through a world of whins!
And when, these perils past, thou seemest *dead*,[11]
    And hope'st a half—O woe, the ball goes crooked,
Making thy foe just one more hole ahead,
    Surely a consummation all too sad,
Without that sneering devilish 'Never lookit,'
    The kind amen of the opposing cad.

VII. HIGH OR EDEN HOLE.

The shelly pit is cleared at one fell blow,
    A stroke to be remembered, e'en in dreams;
    For genius golfy no such other greens
Such hazards have, such tempting bunkers show.
'Willy, my spoon!' for now he must take heed on
    How to play; five yards on either side
    Must land in bunker or th' insidious tide.
'Allow for wind!' says Will—too late; 'tis in the Eden!
Drawn by the club, and carried by the wind,
The ball is lost, the Fates are most unkind.

VIII. OR SHORT HOLE.

A short, enticing, long or short spoon[12] stroke
On wind depending—blow it to or from;
    Perchance 'tis done in *one* immortal go.
    The odds are long, but who, ah, who shall know
How soon a smile or frown Fate may provoke?
From shortened spoon the gutta flies, see! see!
    Straight for the hole, but fifteen yards is past;
    The daintier driver with club well grassed
Is short—the hole is halved in three.
    'Who's never up is never in,'
    The timid putter[13] never yet did win.

IX. OR END HOLE.

That green perspective vista is the line
    On which we strive to keep, but frequent fail,
    When to far right the golfer may bewail
The tee, from which he heeled his ball that time.
Whinned beyond ken, lost at the very last,
    He turneth at the ninth—three holes behind,
    Yet to pull up he must. Genius of golf, be kind;

He may be dormy[14] ere the burn be passed.
So in the midst of life, when we may think we've lost,
We struggle on, and pass the winning-post.

[1] A well-known golf-club maker.
[2] In those days the Union Parlour was the golfer's club-house.
[3] Caddie, a club-carrier.
[4] Sand-pits occur in various places throughout the Links, and are called bunkers.
[5] The tee is the spot near each hole from which the ball is struck off for the next.
[6] Cleek, a club with an iron head, for sending a ball out of difficulties.
[7] Sandy Pirie was a well-known caddie.
[8] The bunker into which a former Principal of St Andrews University frequently drove his ball.
[9] Tom Morris, the well-known and respected custodier of the Links.
[10] An iron-headed club for extracting the ball from sand or other 'hazards.'
[11] When a ball lies near enough to the hole to ensure its being holed next shot, it is said to be dead.
[12] Short spoon, one of the golfer's clubs, used for driving short or 'quarter' strokes.
[13] The putter is the short club used for holing the ball; and as putts frequently fall short of the hole, the axiom has arisen, 'Never up, never in.'
[14] When one of the players or sets of players has gained as many holes as there are holes yet to play in the round or match, he cannot lose, and is therefore said to be dormy.

THE PEERLESS ONE.

Hast thou ne'er marked, in festal hall,
    Amidst the lights that shone,
Some one who beamed more bright than all—
    Some gay—some glorious one!
Some one who, in her fairy lightness,
    As through the hall she went and came;
And her intensity of brightness,
    As ever her eyes sent out their flame,
Was almost foreign to the scene;
    Gay as it was with beauty beaming,

Through which she moved: a gemless queen,
  A creature of a different seeming
From others of a mortal birth—
An angel sent to walk the earth!

Oh, stranger, if thou e'er hast seen
  And singled such a one,
And if thou hast enraptured been—
  And felt thyself undone;
If thou hast sighed for such a one,
  Till thou wert sad with fears;
If thou hast gazed on such a one,
  Till thou wert blind with tears;
If thou hast sat obscure, remote,
  In corner of the hall,
Looking from out thy shroud of thought
  Upon the festival;
Thine eye through all the misty throng
  Drawn by that peerless light,
As traveller's steps are led along
  By wildfire through the night:
Then, stranger, haply dost thou know
The joy, the rapture, and the woe,
Which in alternate tides of feeling,
Now thickening quick, now gently stealing
Throughout this lone and hermit breast,
That festal night, my soul possess'd.

Oh! she was fairest of the fair
  And brightest of the bright;
And there was many a fair one there,
  That joyous festal night.
A hundred eyes on her were bent,
  A hundred hearts beat high;

It was a thing of ravishment,
   O God! to meet her eye!
But 'midst the many who looked on,
   And thought she was divine,
Oh, need I say that there were none
   Who gazed with gaze like mine:
The rest were like the crowd who look
   All idly up to heaven,
And who can see no wonder there
   At either morn or even;
But I was like the wretch embound
Deep in a dungeon underground,
Who only sees through grating high
One small blue fragment of the sky,
Which ever, both at noon and night,
Shows but one starlet shining bright,
Down on the darkness of his place
With cheering and unblenching grace;
The very darkness of my woe
Made her to me more brightly show.

At length the dancing scene was changed
   To one of calmer tone,
And she her loveliness arranged
   Upon fair Music's throne.
Soft silence fell on all around,
   Like dew on summer flowers;
Bright eyes were cast upon the ground
   Like daisies bent with showers.
And o'er that drooping, stilly scene
A voice rose gentle and serene,
   A voice as soft and slow
As might proceed from angel's tongue,

If angel's heart were sorrow wrung,
   And wished to speak its woe.

The song was one of those old lays
   Of mingled gloom and gladness,
Which first the tides of joy can raise,
   Then still them down to sadness;
A strain in which pure joy doth borrow
The very air and gait of sorrow.
And sorrow takes as much alloy
From the rich sparkling ore of joy.
Its notes, like hieroglyphic thing
Spoke more than they seemed meant to sing.
I could have lain my life's whole round
Entranced upon that billowy sound,
Nought touching, tasting, seeing, hearing,
And knowing nothing, nothing fearing,
Like Indian dreaming in his boat,
As he down waveless stream doth float.
But pleasure's tide ebbs always fast,
And these were joys too loved to last.

There was but one long final swell,
   Of full melodious tone,
And all into a cadence fell,
   And was in breathing gone.
And she too went: and thus have gone
   All—all I ever loved;
At first too fondly doted on,
   But soon—too soon removed.
Thus early from each pleasant scene
   There ever has been reft
The summer glow, the pride of green,
   And but brown autumn left.

And oh, what is this cherished term,
    This tenancy of clay,
When that which gave it all its charms
    Has smiled—and passed away?
A chaplet whence the flowers are fallen,
A shrine from which the god is stolen!

ON THE MISSES THREIPLAND OF FINGASK GOING TO SEE THE QUEEN AT BLAIR.

In old Fingask a curtained vision gave,
Methought, the last sad Stuart from his grave.
He viewed the place with melancholy eyes,
Then thus outspoke his soul in painful sighs:
'O house, that once held loyalty so dear,
Can it then be that you must also veer?
Must you, the last supporters of our claim,
Turn votaries of usurping Brunswick's name,
Leaving the memory of your rightful kings
Huddled aside amongst old outworn things?
Alas! 'tis so, your acts the case declare
E'er since you joined the vulgar throng at Blair.
Now, now indeed is *Eighty-eight* complete,
Since even Eliza bows at Vicky's feet.
Now has our grief-cup come to overflow
With this one last and bitterest drop of woe!
Degenerate Threiplands, in your shame exult,
But know that yet must come the pangs of guilt,
The historic beauty of your name is gone,
Now undistinguished where it stood alone;
This will the torpid conscience soon awake,
And cause your souls with strong remorse to shake.

But all too late, for what could then restore
The spotless honour that you held of yore!
While sobs convulsive heaved his shadowy breast;
Oh sad, sad ruin!' Here the spectre ceased,
Then melted slowly in a dim moonbeam,
And I awoke to find it was *no dream*.
1847.

THE ANNUITANT'S ANSWER.

IN REPLY TO OUTRAM'S 'ANNUITY.'

The Annuity, which was written by the late George Outram, and appeared in that unique collection of humorous verse entitled *Legal Lyrics*, was sung with great effect by Mr Peter Fraser, a well-known Edinburgh wit. The song portrays the despondency, and finally the despair of an individual who, having sold an annuity to an elderly dame, in hopes, doubtless, of her speedy release from life and all its cares and woes, finds her calling year after year for her cash, and to all appearance wearing a charmed existence. She breaks her arm and encounters various other casualties without, however, being affected in health; and to an advanced age she 'calls for her annuity.'

Having held its own for some years, it occurred to Dr Robert Chambers that an *Answer* to the *Annuity* ought to appear as given by the old annuitant herself, in vindication of her right to live as long as she could; and accordingly he penned the following verses, which were sung for the first time by Mrs R. Chambers, on the occasion of a dinner-party at 1 Doune Terrace, comprising some of the chief notables of Edinburgh. At this memorable symposium everything and everybody was Scotch. The dishes consisted of cockie-leekie broth, crappit heads, haggis, sheep's-head, &c.; whilst the guests comprised Sir Adam Ferguson, Sheriff Gordon, Professor Aytoun, D. O. Hill, Peter Fraser, James Ballantine, &c. The only lady at the table was the hostess, Mrs Robert Chambers.

It had been arranged beforehand that certain songs from *Legal Lyrics* were to be sung by gentlemen of the party, the *Annuity* being apportioned to Mr Fraser, who sung it in his usual happy manner. 'Now,' said the host, 'I call upon my wife to respond;' whereupon, to the delight, and no less to the surprise of the company, Mrs Chambers sung the *Answer*.

My certy, but it sets him weel,
    Sae vile a tale to tell o' me!
I never could suspect the chiel
    O' sic disingenuity.
I'll no be ninety-four for lang,
My health is far frae being strang;
And he'll mak profit, richt or wrang,
    Ye'll see, by this annuity!

My friends, ye weel can understand,
    This warld is fu' o' roguerie;
And ane meets folk on ilka hand,
    To rug, and rive, and pu' at ye.
I thought that this same man o' law
Wad save my siller frae them a';
And sae I gave the whillywha*
    The hale,† for an annuity.

He says the bargain lookit fair,
    And sae to him I'm sure 'twad be;
I gat my hunder pound a year,
    And he could weel allow it, tae.
And does he think, the deevil's limb,
Although I lookit auld and grim,
I was to die to pleasure him,
    And squash my braw annuity?

The year had scarcely turned its back,
    When he was irking to be free—

* Wheedler.   † Whole.

A fule! the thing to undertak,
  And then sae sune to rue it ye!
I've never been at peace sinsyne,
Nae wonder that sae sair I crine,
It's just through terror that I tine
  My life for my annuity.

He's twice had poison in my kale,
  And sax times in my cup o' tea;
I could unfauld a shocking tale
  O' something in a cruet, tae.
His arms he ance flang round my neck,
I thought it was to show respeck—
He only meant to gie a check,
  Not *for*, but *to* th' annuity.

Said ance to me an honest man:
  'Try an insurance companie;
Ye'll find it an effective plan,
  Protection to secure it ye.
Ten pounds a year—ye weel can spare 't—
Be that wi' Peter Fraser* wair'd;
His office, syne, will be a guard
  For you and your annuity!'

I gaed at ance and spak to Pate,
  'Bout a five-hunder policy—
And 'Haith,' says he, 'ye are nae blate—
  I maist could clamahewit† ye!
Wi' that chiel's fingers at the knife,
What chance ha'e ye o' length o' life?
Gae to the deil, ye silly wife,
  Wi' you and your annuity!'

---

* A well-known Edinburgh wit, and agent for a life insurance company at the time the *Annuitant's Answer* was written.   † Strike.

The Procurator-fiscal's now
    The only friend that I can see,
And it's sma' thing that he can do
    To help my sair anxiety:
But honest Maurice * has agreed,
That, gin the villain does the deed,
He'll swing at Libberton's-Wynd-head †
    For me and my annuity.

THE PRISONER OF SPEDLINS.

To Edinburgh, to Edinburgh,
    The Jardine he maun ride;
He locks the gates behind him,
    For lang he means to bide.

And he, nor any of his train,
    While minding thus to flit,
Thinks of the weary prisoner,
    Deep in the castle pit.

They were not gane a day, a day,
    A day but barely four,
When neighbours spoke of dismal cries
    Were heard frae Spedlins Tower.

They mingled wi' the sigh of trees,
    And the thud-thud o' the lin;
But nae ane thocht 'twas a deein' man
    That made that eldrich din.

---

* Maurice Lothian, then procurator-fiscal (that is, public prosecutor) for the county of Edinburgh.
† Formerly the place of execution in Edinburgh.

At last they mind the gipsy loon,
    In dungeon lay unfed ;
But ere the castle key was got,
    The gipsy loon was dead.

They found the wretch stretch'd out at length
    Upon the cold cold stone,
With starting eyes and hollow cheek,
    And arms peeled to the bone!

.   .   .   .

Now Spedlins is an eerie house,
    For oft at mirk midnight
The wail of Porteous' starving cry
    Fills a' that house wi' fright.

' O let me out, O let me out,
    Sharp hunger cuts me sore ;
If ye suffer me to perish so,
    I'll haunt you evermore !'

O sad sad was the Jardine then,
    His heart was sorely smit ;
Till he could wish himself had been
    Left in that deadly pit.

But ' Cheer ye,' cried his lady fair,
    ' 'Tis purpose makes the sin ;
And where the heart has had no part,
    God holds his creature clean.'

Then Jardine sought a holy man
    To lay that vexing sprite ;
And for a week that holy man
    Was praying day and night.

And all that time in Spedlins house
    Was held a solemn fast,
Till the cries waxed low, and the boglebs
    In the deep Red Sea was cast.

   .   .   .   .   .

There lies a Bible in Spedlins ha',
    And while it there shall lie,
Nae Jardine can tormented be
    With Porteous' starving cry.

But Applegarth's an altered man—
    He is no longer gay;
The thought o' Porteous clings to him
    Unto his dying day.

IN THE ALBUM AT KINNAIRD CASTLE, PERTHSHIRE.

Laud to the ladies of Fingask
For their self-devoting task;
Building up the crumbling walls
Which contained their fathers' halls;
Taking a new lease from time
For this antique tower sublime,
Raised at first by monarch's hand,
As a safeguard to the land;
Where another monarch came,
O'er these braes to chase the game,
While St James's and Whitehall
Missed his merry festival.

Monument of ancient days
Better never could you raise ;
Here the sullen battlement,
Loop-holes whence the dart was sent,
Pondrous grille behind the door,
The once archèd massy more,
Hall where noble guests have sate
Round bold barons holding state ;
Elsewhere accommodation small,
But strength to hold made up for all.
Still, too, you may beneath the place,
The stately terraced garden trace,
And in the neighbouring bosky dell,
Imbibe the lymph from Spinky Well,
Where, as old legends fondly prove,
A knight once died for lady's love.

Go on, dear ladies, and not rest,
Till all Time's wrongs you have redressed,
And Threipland's name shall ever be
Inwoven in my minstrelsie.

1854.

'ALL RIGHT.'

Tune—*Packington's Pound.*

While the coach stops a moment, a cup of brown ale
To the chilly *outsides* is a welcome regale ;
Mine host hands it smiling, and when it's drunk up,
He takes back the sixpence along with the cup :
   Not a little cares he
   For the jeopardy
That may be on the cards for the passengers three ;

He slips to his pocket the silver so bright,
And passes the word to the coachman—'*All Right!*'

They may drive anywhere, may lose life or break limb,
No matter what happens, 'tis all right to him,
He has served out his liquor, and taken his cash,
He stands unaffected, though all go to smash;
    Had the sixpence proved bad,
    Or none to be had,
  In that case alone would mine host have been sad;
But the coin was forthcoming, and honour was bright,
And so he reported to coachy—'*All Right!*'

If we look round the world, I think we shall see
That many are much in the same way as he;
Give them all that they wish for, concede every claim,
And what haps to others will ne'er trouble them:
    They wish ill to none,
    But then there is *one*
  On whose fortunes exclusive their thoughts ever run;
When *that one* is served, they look round with delight,
And, though friends may be sinking, their cry is—'*All Right!*'

The shopman will tell you his wares are so fine,
And he takes but five shillings for what is worth nine;
He advises his customers, quite as their friend,
On goods so good-cheap very freely to spend;
    His words are so nice,
    That they take his advice,
  And for all they purchase they only pay thrice;
He sees them depart with a bow so polite,
And pockets their money, and thinks it—*All Right!*

The lawyer so wily will push on your plea,
But for every new motion expects a big fee;
He bids you have courage, nor heed how you bleed,
For, if you but pay well, you're sure to succeed:
    Long, long the delay,
    But at length comes the day
  When to all your great hopes the wise judges say nay:
You're left just enough to pay off Master Bite,
Who receipts your last doit with an easy—'*All Right!*'

You're ill, and the doctor attends at your call,
Feels your pulse, and looks grave, but says nothing at all;
You think him so knowing—he's only demure—
And expect every day he will bring you a cure:
    He tries all his skill
    With blister and pill,
  But it all ends in nothing but swelling his bill;
At last you march off, like a poor mortal wight,
And he slams to the door of your hearse with—'*All Right!*

The would-be M.P. comes with smiles and with bows,
Caresses your children, and kisses your spouse,
He's full of professions—will do this and that—
And to all your opinions his own are so pat:
    You think you have got
    A sound patriot,
  And do less you cannot than give him your vote
In the House he sees things in a quite different light,
The fellow has choused you—no matter—*All Right!*

The man who has thousands on thousands in store,
And still every year adds a few thousands more,

Who feasts in a palace, from plate, every day,
With the world all around him so pleasant and gay—
        He sees his poor neighbour
        Oppressed with his labour,
So unlike the old days of the pipe and the tabor,
He's perhaps no bad fellow, but still to his sight
The arrangement seems perfect—his cry is—'*All Right!*'

In short, with all human the rule must still hold—
Let a gemman, for instance, have honours and gold;
Give a lady that handsomest, landedest squire,
Whom all other ladies most praise and admire;
        Or give to a child
        A platter well piled,
While others are starving and crying like wild;
Each fortunate elf will be satisfied quite
With the course of events, and declare it—*All Right!*

ON SEEING SOME WORK-HORSES IN A PARK ON A SUNDAY.

    'Tis Sabbath-day, the poor man walks
      Blithe from his cottage door,
    And to his prattling young ones talks
      As they skip on before.

    The father is a man of joy,
      From his week's toil released;
    And jocund is each little boy
      To see his father pleased.

    But, looking to a field at hand,
      Where the grass grows rich and high,
    A no less merry Sabbath band
      Of horses met my eye.

Poor skinny beasts! that go all week
  With loads of earth and stones,
Bearing, with aspect dull and meek,
  Hard work and cudgell'd bones;

But now let loose to rove athwart
  The farmer's clover lea,
With whisking tails, and jump and snort,
  They speak a clumsy glee.

Lolling across each other's necks,
  Some look like brothers dear;
Others are full of flings and kicks,
  Antics uncouth and queer.

One tumbles wild from side to side,
  With hoofs tossed to the sun,
Cooling his old gray seamy hide,
  And making dreadful fun.

I thought how pleasant 'twas to see,
  On this bright Sabbath-day,
Man and his beasts alike set free
  To take some harmless play;

And how their joys were near the same—
  The same in show, at least—
Hinting that we may sometimes claim
  Too much above the beast.

If like in joys, beasts surely must
  Be like in sufferings too,
And we can not be right or just
  To treat them as we do.

Thus did God's day serve as a span
    All things to bind together,
And make the humble brute to man
    A patient pleading brother.

Oh, if to us *one precious thing*,
    And not to them, is given,
Kindness to them will be a wing
    To carry it on to heaven!

'UNDER TRUSTEES.'

TUNE—*The Jolly Young Waterman.*

Oh have you ne'er heard of a worthy Scotch gentleman,
    Laird of that ilk, and the chief of his name,
Who not many years since, attaining majority,
    Heir to some thousands of acres became?
He lived so well, and he spent so merrily,
The people all came to his house so readily,
    And he made all things in it so much as you please,
    And he made all things in it so much as you please,
That this gentleman soon was put under trustees.

Oh never till then had our worthy Scotch gentleman
    Lived for a day as his taste did incline,
There never were wanting some plaguy good fellows
    To rattle his pheasants and tipple his wine.
He kept a pack, which the county delighted in,
He gave charming balls, and the ladies invited in;
    Oh he never knew what was a moment of ease,
    Oh he never knew what was a moment of ease,
Till snug he had placed himself under trustees.

Being too truly now a Distressed Agriculturist,
    No one expects him to play the great man;
He is sure of whatever he needs in this world,
    For creditors wish him to live while he can.
Rents may fall, but that doesn't trouble him;
Banks may break, but that cannot hobble him;
    At the cares of this sad life he coolly may sneeze,
    At the cares of this sad life he coolly may sneeze,
Who only will put himself under trustees!

Subscriptions come round for election-committees,
    New churches, infirmaries, soup for the poor;
Our worthy Scotch gentleman gives his best wishes,
    But of course the collectors ne'er darken his door.
He never is called to look a paper in,
To get up a cup to huntsman or whipper-in;
    Oh who would be *fashing* with matters like these,
    Oh who would be *fashing* with matters like these,
A gentleman known to be under trustees?

When any good neighbour, hard up for the wherewithal,
    Looks for some friend who is likely to lend,
Our worthy Scotch gentleman never need care at all—
    He's not the man who the matter can mend.
In short, all others have something crossing them,
On beds of trouble are always tossing them;
    But only the Income-Tax truly can tease,
    But only the Income-Tax truly can tease,
A gentleman snugly put under trustees.

ELSINORE.

TUNE—*Excelsior.*

A small but very merry party assembled at Woodhill, Forfarshire, in May 1859, under the hospitality of James Miln, Esq. It included Patrick Arkley, Esq., one of the sheriffs of Mid-Lothian; Alexander Hay Miln, Esq., of Woodhill; and Dr Robert Chambers. Mr Arkley had come with the design of chiefly spending his time in fishing in the burn called the Elsinore, which runs past Woodhill, but was diverted from his purpose in order to accompany his companions on sundry excursions about the neighbourhood. His returning to Edinburgh, *re infectâ*, together with some considerations as to the smallness of the burn on which his sanguinary thoughts had been bent, gave rise to the following jocular verses:

    A sheriff came to sweet Woodhill,
    Thinking to try his angling skill;
    All proper implements had he,
    He viewed the fated burn with glee,
                The Elsinore!

    He saw it all in fancy's dream,
    A basket filled, a ravaged stream,
    Or, that his landlord might not grieve,
    He thought how many he would leave
                In Elsinore!

    To favour the intended sack,
    The miller dammed the water back;
    The trouts lay at the barrier quakin',
    And felt themselves already taken
                In Elsinore!

Poor little burnie, what a plight
You lay in, all that summer night,
While Arkley's slumbers were enlaced
With visions of thy wrack and waste,
     Dear Elsinore!

Yet, after all the botheration,
And 'dreadful note of preparation,'
The day passed o'er on golden wings,
And Arkley thought of other things
     Than Elsinore.

He could not be upon the Laws,
Examining its ancient wa's,
And lunching afterwards with Neish,
Yet pay attention to the fish
     Of Elsinore.

Day softened into moony eve,
Woodhill next morning he must leave,
He wished and wished his soul away,
But could not touch the finny prey
     In Elsinore!

Morn came—he went—the trouts drew breath,
Respited from the doom of death;
The miller thought 'twas all a sham,
And coolly went, and loosed the dam
     Of Elsinore.

To Arkley now remains alone
The thought of what he might have done,

Or, taking hope's propitious view,
The thought of what he yet may do,
    In Elsinore.

Fair stream, be thou the happy goal
Of Arkley's piscatorial soul;
A type of his potential mood,
A thing that might, could, would, or should
    Be Elsinore!

1859.

LIFE INSURANCE.

Come now, my friend, and do not stare,
 And listen to my strain a bit;
I wish to make you just aware
 Of something for your benefit:
As yet you say, upon your life
 You have not got a policy,
'Tis downright treason to your wife,
 I wish you would your folly see,
  And think upon insurance,
  Oh, think of life insurance;
   If you will not cast in your lot,
  You'll vex me past endurance.

Our office is for soundness known,
 The steadfast Perpendicular;
And when you would be choosing one,
 You can't be too particular.

Our 'cumulated fund appears
   Increasing at a steady rate;
A bonus every seven years,
   And yet our premiums moderate.
     Then think upon insurance,
     Our office of insurance;
       If you will not cast in your lot,
       You 'll vex me past endurance.

We 'll say you 're thirty next birthday,
   You ne'er had epilepsy, sir,
Insanity, gout, hernia,
   Consumption, or dyspepsy, sir.
Your medical attendant says
   You 're come of healthy parentage;
You 've lived in Britain all your days,
   And are of your apparent age;
     Then, oh, my friend, insurance,
     Think, think of life insurance;
       If you will not cast in your lot,
       You 'll vex me past endurance.

Your present state of health is good,
   With healthy occupation, sir;
Your well-formed bellows-chest has stood
   The doctor's auscultation, sir.
No hazard in your way of life;
   You 're neither log nor cripple, sir;
Last year you took yourself a wife;
   You 're moderate in your tipple, sir;
     A model for insurance,
     First-rate for life insurance!
       Oh, if you 'll not cast in your lot,
       You 'll vex me past endurance.

Pray don't forget, though healthy yet,
   You 're subject to mortality :
The life of man we only can
   Foretell in the totality.
The first year's premium being paid,
   You may demise to-morrow, sir,
And then your widow will not need
   To either beg or borrow, sir :
      She 's saved by life insurance ;
      Oh, noble life insurance !
        Oh, if you 'll not cast in your lot,
      You 'll vex me past endurance.

But say you 've got a policy,
   Or even more than one of them,
You may another take from me,
   You 'll thrive beneath a ton of them.
One ought to add a thousand pounds,
   Each new responsibility ;
It is a duty has no bounds,
   But just a man's ability.
      Then, oh, once more, insurance,
      Oh, think of life insurance !
        Oh, if you 'll not cast in your lot,
      You 'll vex me past endurance.

Long, long ago there was a man,
   Who called himself knight-errant, sir,
Who, as the ladies' friend did rove,
   Protecting them from tyrants, sir :
But, ladies, I 'm your best friend now,
   As good as any lover t' ye,

For all my object 's to endow,
  And save you, dears, from poverty.
    Then help me with insurance,
    Oh, help on life insurance;
      If husbands not cast in their lot,
    Declare them past endurance.

1859.

THE END.

www.ingramcontent.com/pod-product-compliance
Lightning Source LLC
Chambersburg PA
CBHW031605110426
42742CB00037B/1262